Animal Offspring

Bears and Their Cubs

by Linda Tagliaferro

Consulting Editor: Gail Saunders-Smith, Ph.D.

Consultant: Klari Lea, President
The American Bear Association
Orr, Minnesota

Capstone
press

Mankato, Minnesota

Pebble Plus is published by Capstone Press
151 Good Counsel Drive, P.O. Box 669, Mankato, Minnesota 56002
http://www.capstonepress.com

1 2 3 4 5 6 09 08 07 06 05 04

Library of Congress Cataloging-in-Publication Data
Tagliaferro, Linda.
Bears and their cubs/by Linda Tagliaferro.
p.cm.—(Pebble plus, Animal offspring)
Contents: Bears—Cubs—Growing up—Watch bears grow.
Includes bibliographical references and index.
ISBN 0-7368-2387-5 (hardcover)
1. Bear cubs—Juvenile literature. 2. Bears—Juvenile literature. 3. Parental behavior in animals—Juvenile literature. [1. Bears. 2. Animals—Infancy. 3. Parental behavior in animals.] I. Title. II. Series.
QL737.C27T324 2004
599.78—dc21   2003008488

Editorial Credits
Sarah L. Schuette, editor; Kia Adams, series designer; Kelly Garvin and Deirdre Barton, photo researchers;
    Karen Risch, product planning editor

Photo Credits
Bruce Coleman Inc./Charles G. Summers, 5; Leonard Lee Rue, 7, 20 (left)
Corbis/John W. Herbst, 10–11
Erwin & Peggy Bauer, 1, 8–9, 20 (right)
Minden Pictures/Matthias Breiter, 17; Michio Hoshino, cover; Mitsuaki Iwago, 12–13
Robin Brandt, 21 (both)
Tom & Pat Leeson, 15, 18–19

Note to Parents and Teachers

The Animal Offspring series supports national science standards related to life science. This book describes and illustrates bears and their cubs. The images support early readers in understanding the text. The repetition of words and phrases helps early readers learn new words. This book also introduces early readers to subject-specific vocabulary words, which are defined in the Glossary section. Early readers may need assistance to read some words and to use the Table of Contents, Glossary, Read More, Internet Sites, and Index/Word List sections of the book.

Word Count: 116
Early-Intervention Level: 13

Table of Contents

Bears

Bears and their cubs
are mammals. Bears have
large bodies and long fur.
Eight types of bears live
in the world.

Male bears are boars.

Female bears are sows.

Boars and sows mate.

Sows usually give birth

to two cubs.

Cubs

Newborn cubs cannot see
or hear until they are
a few days old.

Cubs drink milk from their mother for a few months.

Cubs use their sharp claws
to climb trees.

Growing Up

Mother bears teach
their cubs to hunt and
find food. They learn to
eat fish, fruit, and bugs.

Cubs stand up and play
with each other.

Most cubs stay with their mother for about two years. Then the cubs go to live on their own.

Watch Bears Grow

birth

**adult after three
to five years**

Glossary

boar—a male member of the bear family

cub—a young bear; bear cubs depend on their mothers to feed them and to teach them how to hunt on their own.

mammal—a warm-blooded animal that has a backbone; female mammals have hair or fur and feed milk to their young.

mate—to join together to produce young

sow—a female member of the bear family; sows give birth to cubs.

Read More

Cooper, Jason. *Cub to Grizzly.* Animals Growing Up. Vero Beach, Fla.: Rourke, 2003.

Richardson, Adele D. *Bears: Paws, Claws, and Jaws.* The Wild World of Animals. Mankato, Minn.: Bridgestone Books, 2001.

Welvaert, Scott R. *A Bear in its Den.* Where Do Animals Live? Sioux Falls, S.D.: Lake Street Publishers, 2003.

Internet Sites

FactHound offers a safe, fun way to find Internet sites related to this book. All of the sites on FactHound have been researched by our staff.

Here's how:

1. Visit *www.facthound.com*

2. Type in this special code **0736823875** for age-appropriate sites. Or enter a search word related to this book for a more general search.

3. Click on the Fetch It button.

FactHound will fetch the best sites for you!

Index/Word List